PIANO

Worship & Praise

Complete Collection: Favorites from the 1980s to the 2000s

40 Arrangements of Praise and Worship Favorites

Arranged by **James Koerts**

This collection contains a mix of beloved songs from the '80s through the 2000s that have become standards in many churches, as well as some treasured pieces that will bring back memories of contemporary Christian music from decades past. From the reflective to the upbeat, I have carefully crafted these arrangements to accurately reflect the originals, while infusing creative touches throughout.

James Koerts

Produced by
Alfred Music
P.O. Box 10003
Van Nuys, CA 91410-0003
alfred.com

Printed in USA.

ISBN-10: 1-4706-3601-8
ISBN-13: 978-1-4706-3601-2

Cover Photo
Cheering woman at sunset: © Shutterstock.com / Maridav

Contents

(Approx. Performance Time – 4:00)

Change My Heart, Oh God

Words and Music by Eddie Espinosa
Arr. James Koerts

16
mf
20
24
mp
28
32
p

36
40
a tempo
8va
rit.
f
44
8va
48
mf
51
a tempo
rit.
p
8va

(Approx. Performance Time – 2:15)

Great Is the Lord

Words and Music by
Michael W. Smith and Deborah D. Smith
Arr. James Koerts

Brightly, with energy (♩. = 72)

16
f

19

22

25

28
a tempo
mf
rit.
32
36
f
40
mp
44

48
52
poco a poco cresc.
55
f
58
poco a poco cresc.
61

64
ff
67
70
74
77
8va

(Approx. Performance Time – 2:30)

El Shaddai

Words and Music by Donald Lawrence
Arr. James Koerts

17
4
5

21
5
1 3
3
mp

25

29
3
3 1 2

33
37
41
p
45
mf
49

53
(5)
3
2
3
2 1 2
57
3
3
61
5
8va
3
p
65
5
5
3
69
rit.
5
pp

(Approx. Performance Time – 2:30)

He Is Exalted

Words and Music by Twila Paris
Arr. James Koerts

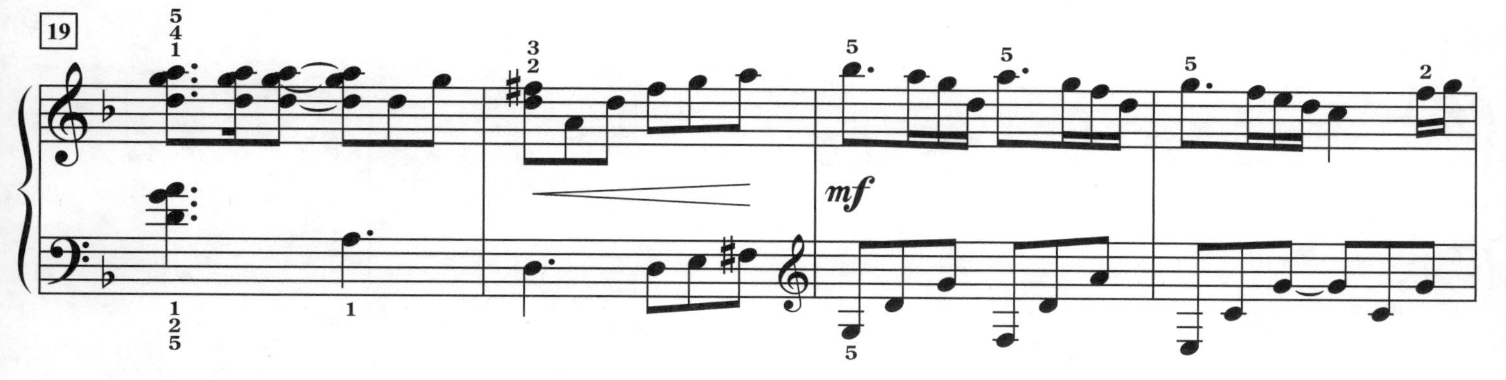
19
mf

23

27

31
f

35
mf
39
44
f
48
52
ff

56
mf

60

64

68
f

72
5
2
2 1 2 3
2
5 3 1 2 1

75
5
2

78
ff
2
2

82
4 2 1
2
mf
ff
1 2 3
5

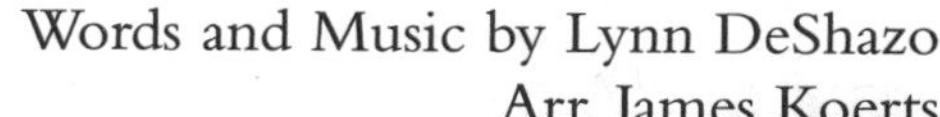

More Precious Than Silver

1980s

Words and Music by Lynn DeShazo
Arr. James Koerts

17
21
8va
25
mf
29
33

37
5
3
2
1
41
4
45
1 3
49
53
1

57
61
65
69
73
f

77
5 2 1 2 1
5 2 1 3 1 2
2 1 2
81
2 1 2 1
85
89
mp
92
8va
p
pp

(Approx. Performance Time – 1:45)

How Majestic Is Your Name

Words and Music by Michael W. Smith
Arr. James Koerts

15
19
23
27
31

34
3
2
1
3
3
5 2 1 2 1 2

38
3
3

42

46

50
mf

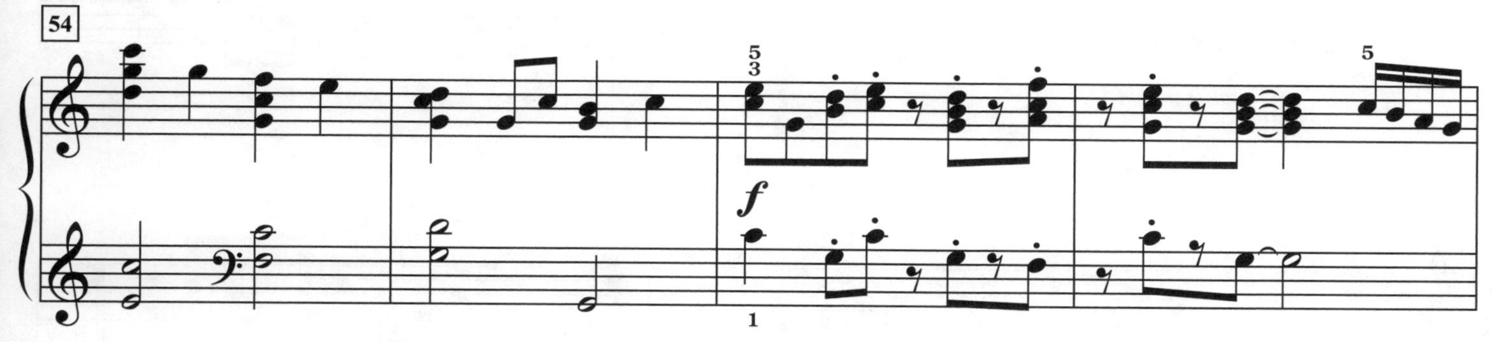
54
f

58

61

(Approx. Performance Time – 3:45)

More Than Wonderful

Words and Music by Lanny Wolfe
Arr. James Koerts

9
11
13
15
17
rit.

A little faster (♩ = 84)
20
23
26
29
32

35
38
41
44
47

49
rit.
51
a tempo
f
53
55
57

59
3
3

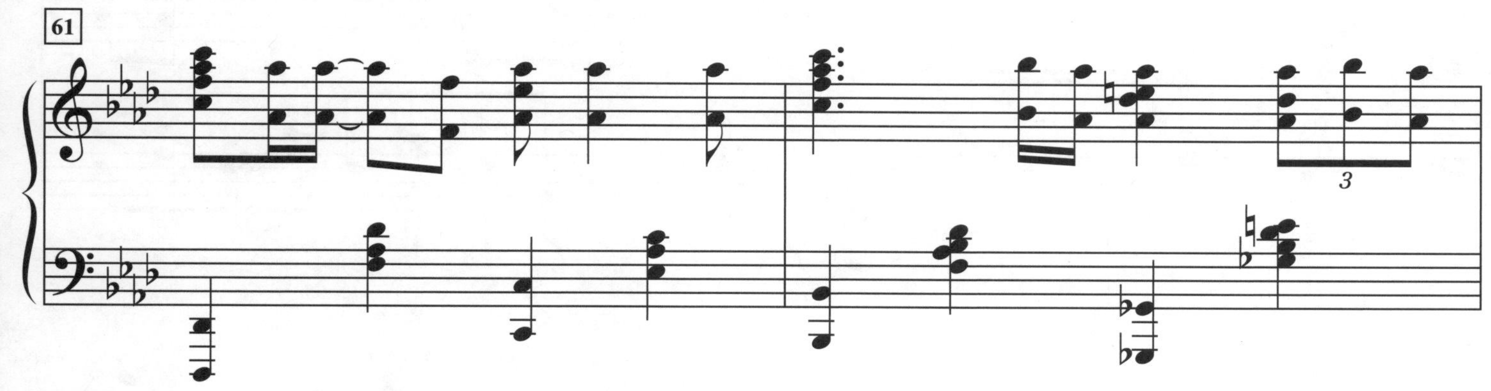
61
3

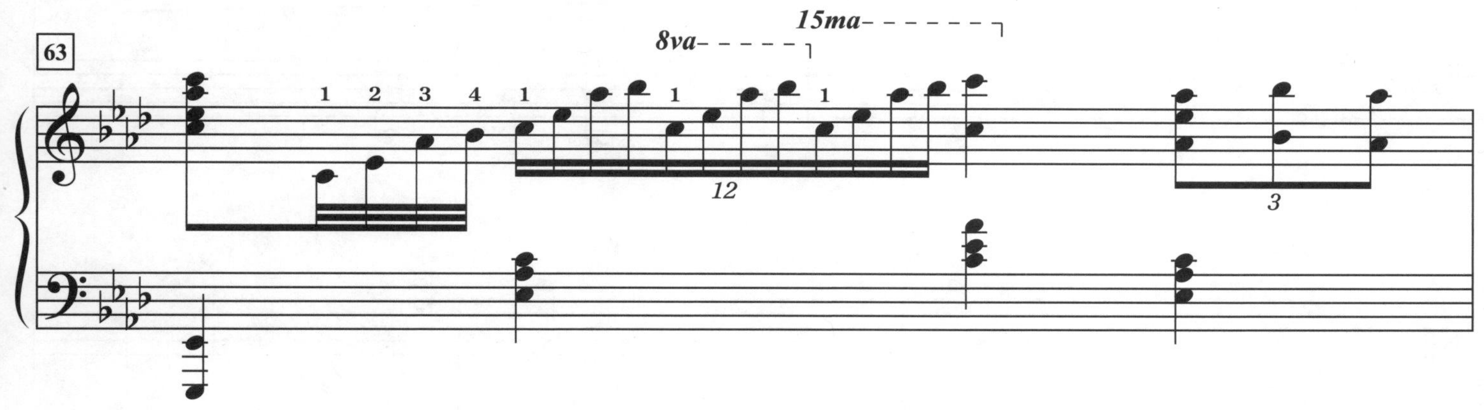
63
15ma
8va
1 2 3 4 1 1 1
12
3

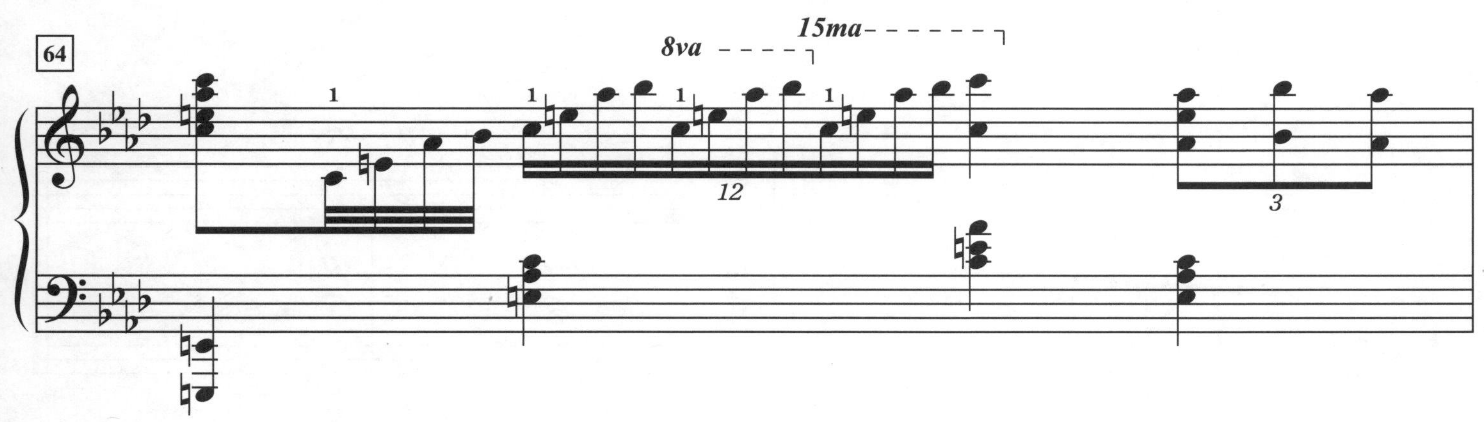
64
15ma
8va
1 1 1 1
12
3

65
8va
15ma
12
3
66
8va
9
3
68
rit.
71
a tempo
mf
74
rit.
mp
p

(Approx. Performance Time – 2:45)

Thank You

Words and Music by Ray Boltz
Arr. James Koerts

18
mp
22
26
30
34

38
42
46
50
mf
54

58
62
66
69
73

77

81
dim.

84
mp
rit.
a tempo
p

88
pp

(Approx. Performance Time – 2:00)

Was It a Morning Like This?

Words and Music by Jim Croegaert
Arr. James Koerts

15
2.
f
19
22
25
28

31
mp
8va
34
38
41
45

48
51
54
57
ff
60
sffz

(Approx. Performance Time – 2:15)

Wonderful, Merciful Savior

Words and Music by
Eric Wyse and Dawn Rodgers
Arr. James Koerts

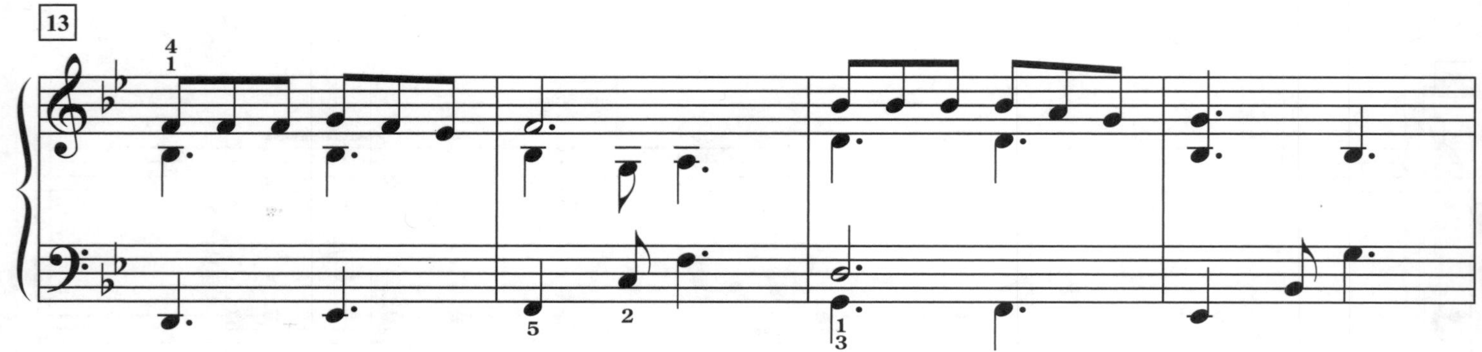

17
21
25
29
33
mf

37
41
45
49
53
f

57
61
mf
65
mp
69
rit.
73
a tempo
rit. e dim.
p
8va

(Approx. Performance Time – 4:15)

Above All

Words and Music by
Paul Baloche and Lenny LeBlanc
Arr. James Koerts

14

17

20

23
mf

26
dim.
29
mp
32
a tempo
rit.
mf
35
38

41

44

47
f

50

53

56
dim.
mp

59
rit.

62
a tempo
dim.
p

(Approx. Performance Time – 3:15)

Better Is One Day

Words and Music by Matt Redman
Arr. James Koerts

1990s

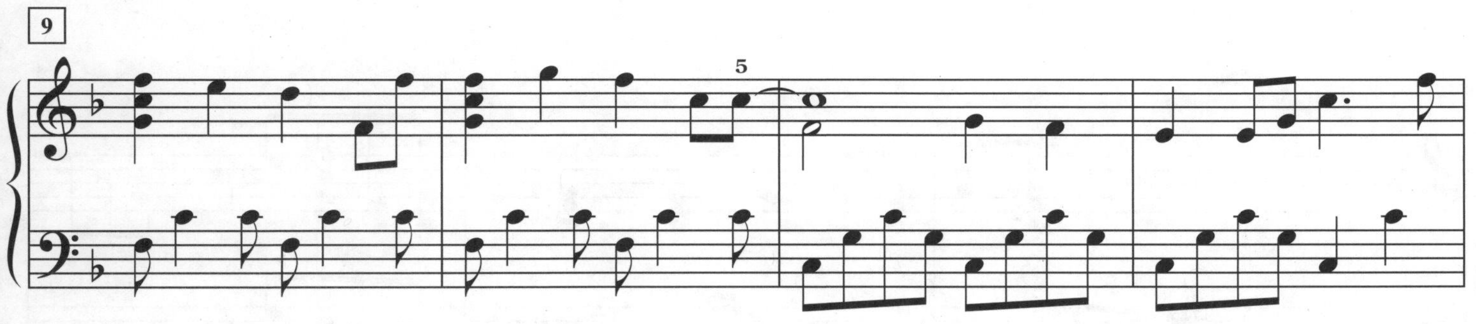

17
21
24
27
30
mf

33
37
41
f
45
49
poco a poco dim.
mp

(Approx. Performance Time – 2:45)

Come, Now Is the Time to Worship

Words and Music by Brian Doerksen
Arr. James Koerts

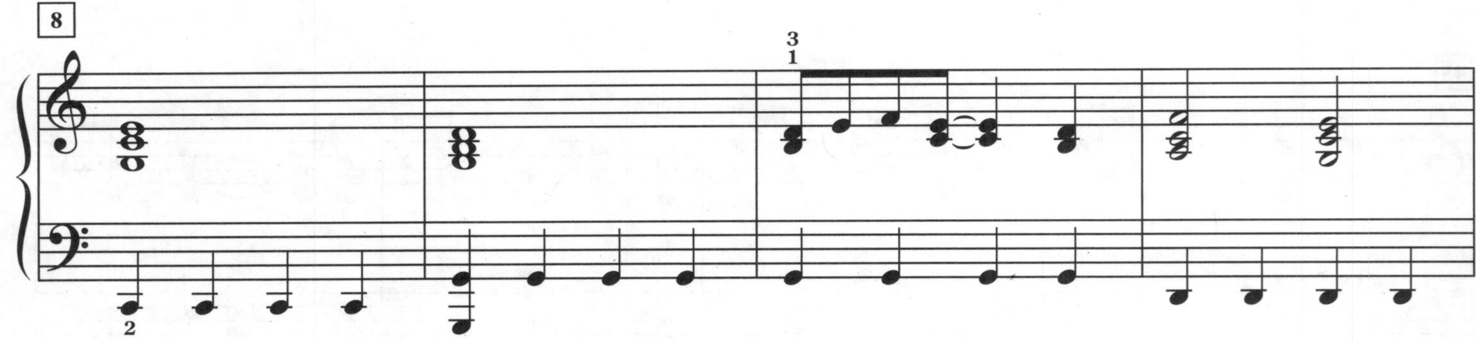

16
20
24
dim.
mf
(mel.)
28
32

54
5
3
1
1
2
f
3
2
1
1
2
3
57
1
2
4
1
2
3
2
1
60
1
2
63
66
1
2

69

72

75
p

78
dim.
rit.
8va
pp

(Approx. Performance Time – 2:30)

Crown Him King of Kings

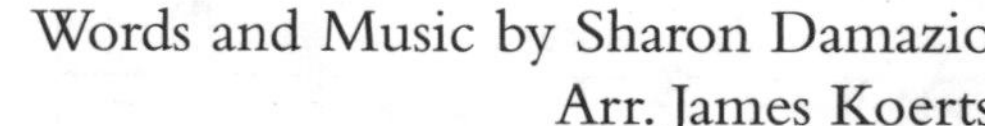

19
23
mf
27
31
rit.
a tempo
f
35

39
ff
43
f
47
rit.
a tempo
50
mf
f
53

(Approx. Performance Time – 2:30)

The Heart of Worship
(When the Music Fades)

Words and Music by Matt Redman
Arr. James Koerts

14
4
5
2
1
2
17
20
4
3
5
2
1
2
23
4
5
26
3

29
mp
33
37
40
43

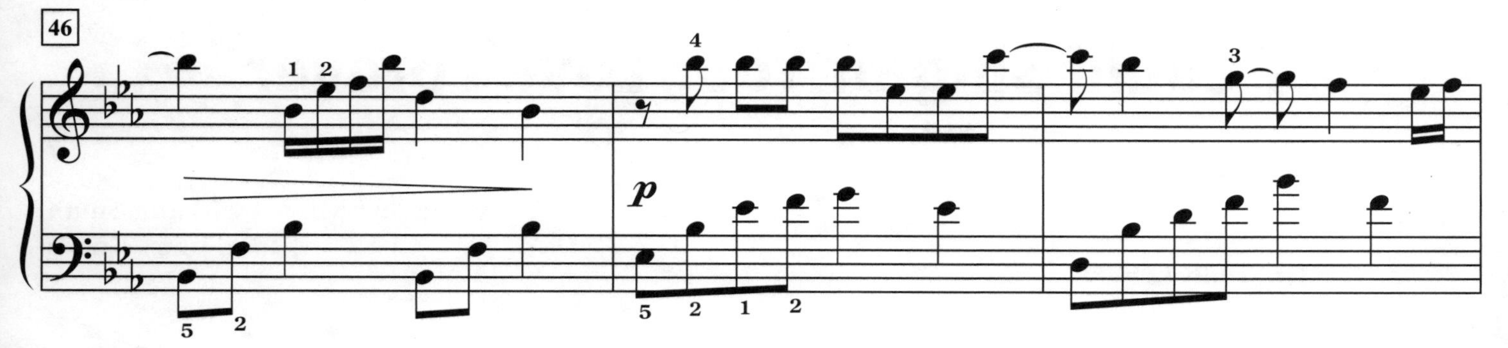

1990s

(Approx. Performance Time – 2:30)

I Could Sing of Your Love Forever

Words and Music by Martin Smith
Arr. James Koerts

13
(4)
2
1
5 2 1 2
16
4
2
1
5
19
mp
22
25

28
32
36
39
42

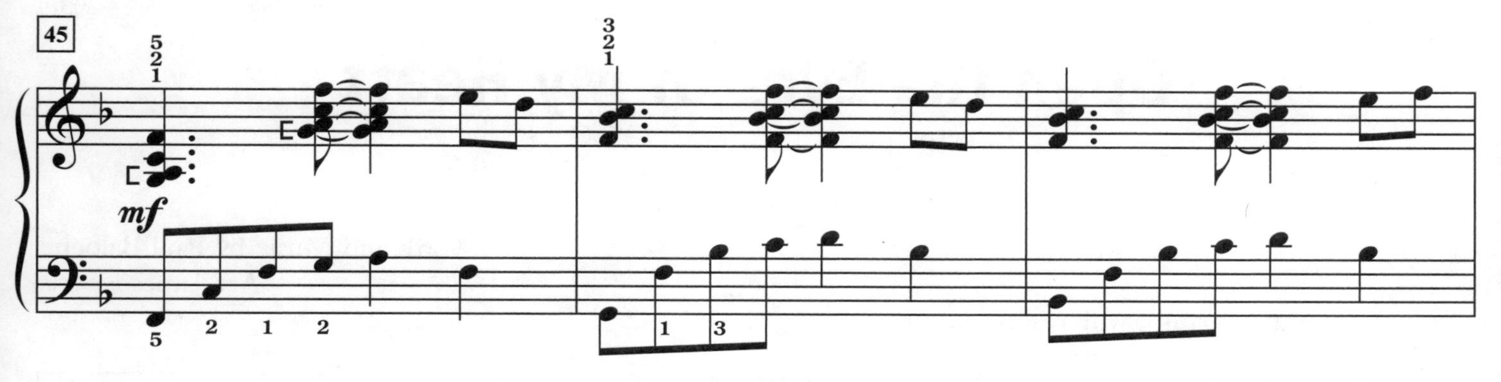
45
mf

48

51
mp

54
rit.

(Approx. Performance Time – 3:30)

Open the Eyes of My Heart

Words and Music by Paul Baloche
Arr. James Koerts

16
20
23
mp
27
31
mf

35
38
f
42
46
p
50

54
mf
58
62
mp
66
69
rit. e dim.
p
8va

(Approx. Performance Time – 3:30)

Shout to the Lord

Words and Music by Darlene Zschech
Arr. James Koerts

16
20
24
27
mf
30

33
36
39
42
mp
46

50
mf
54
57
60
f
63

66
ff
69
72
dim.
75
mp
79
rit.
p

(Approx. Performance Time – 2:30)

We Fall Down

Words and Music by Chris Tomlin
Arr. James Koerts

17
mp
21
25
29
33
mf

37

41

45

49
dim.
rit.
p
8va

(Approx. Performance Time – 4:00)

You Are My All in All

Words and Music by Dennis L. Jernigan
Arr. James Koerts

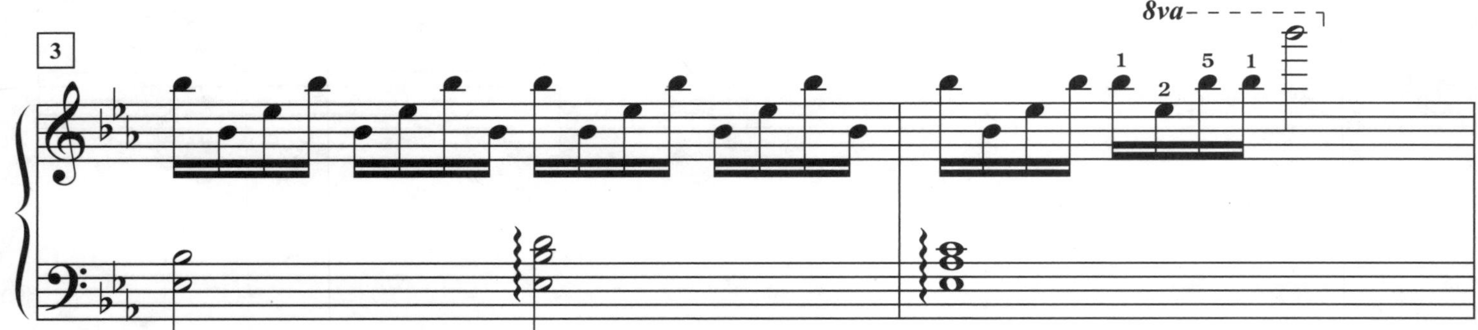

9
mp

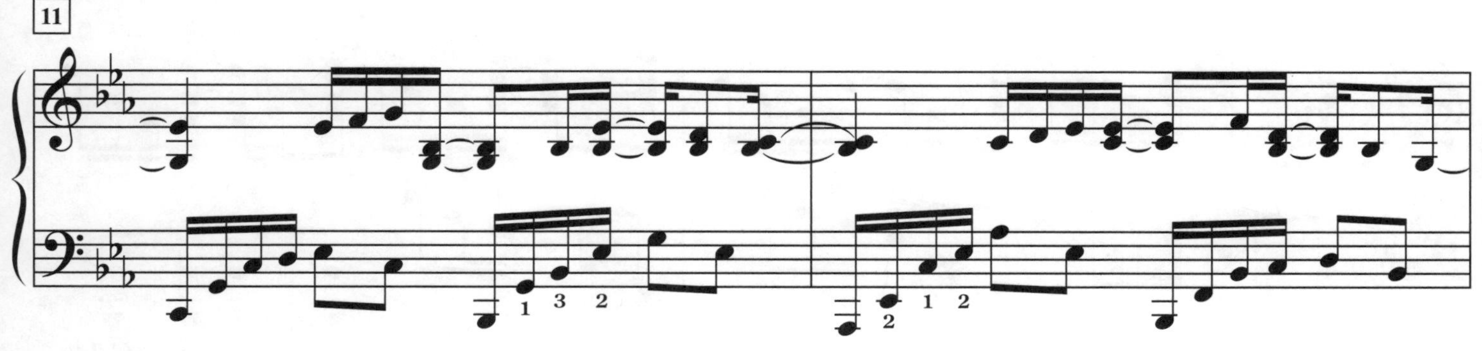
11

13

15

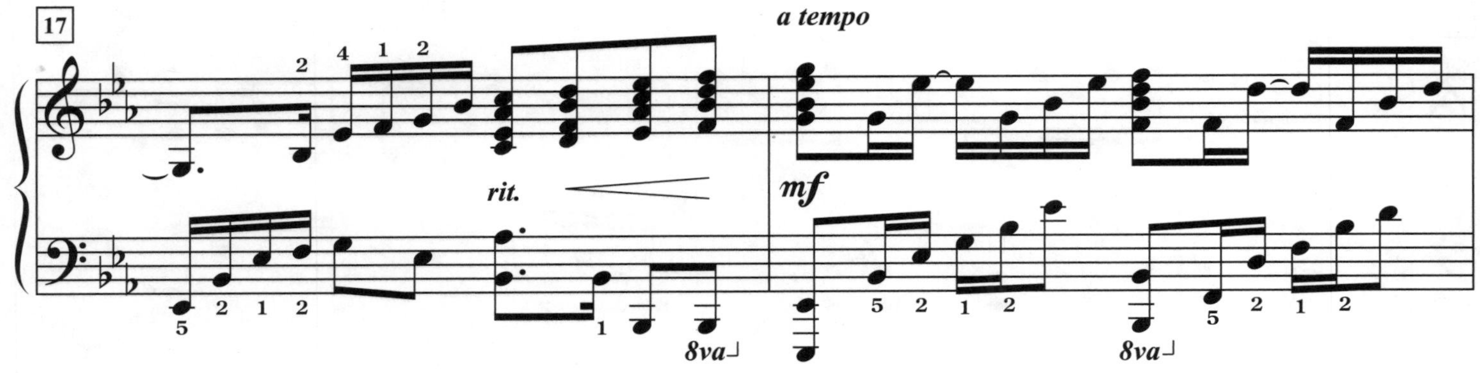
17
a tempo
2 4 1 2
rit.
mf
5 2 1 2
1
8va
5 2 1 2
5 2 1 2
8va

19
5 2 1 2
8va
5 3 2 1 2
5 3 2
8va

21
5 2 1 2
5 2 1 2
8va
5 2
5 2
8va

23
5 2
8va
5 3 2
5 3 2
8va

25

27

29

31

33
1
2
1
2
f
5
2
1
2
35
3
2
1
2
1
2
1
2
37
1
2
39
3
2
1
2
1
2
1
2
41
2

43
2
5 2 1 2
dim.
45
8va
1 2 5 1
mp
47
8va
1 2 5 1
49
3
p
51
rit.

(Approx. Performance Time – 3:00)

Beautiful One

Words and Music by Tim Hughes
Arr. James Koerts

16
20
23
26
29

33
mp
37
41
45
mf
f
49

53
p

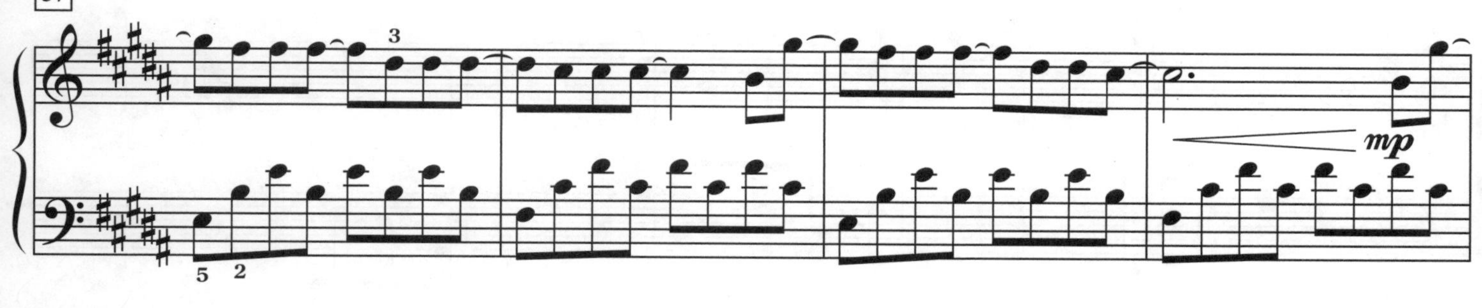
57
mp

61
mf

65
f

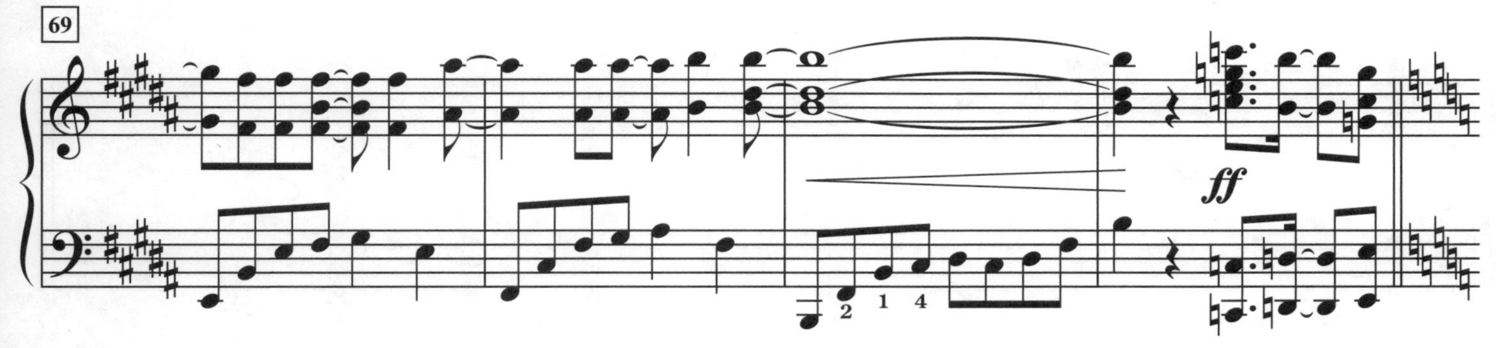
69
ff

73
2 1 2
2
76
2
79
1 2 4 1
6
2
82
1 2 4 1
6
2
85
6
rit.
3
3
1
8va

(Approx. Performance Time – 3:00)

Enough

Words and Music by
Chris Tomlin and Louie Giglio
Arr. James Koerts

Gently, with assurance (♩ = 72)

Early 2000s

15
p
19
23
mp
27
31
mf

34
37
41
45
49
mp
rit.

(Approx. Performance Time – 3:30)

God of Wonders

Words and Music by
Marc Byrd and Steve Hindalong
Arr. James Koerts

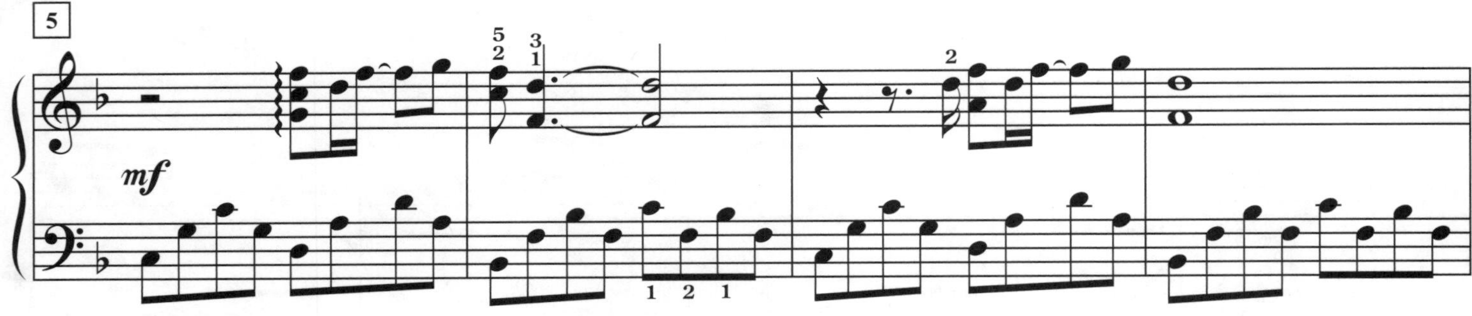

16
19
22
25
mp
29

32
mf
35
38
41
44

47
f
50
53
56
59
mf
rit.

(Approx. Performance Time – 4:00)

Here I Am to Worship
(Light of the World)

Words and Music by Tim Hughes
Arr. James Koerts

17
21
25
mf
29
33
mp

37
41
mf
45
49
53
f

56
59
62
65
68
mf
mp
p

(Approx. Performance Time – 3:45)

How Great Is Our God

Words and Music by
Jesse Reeves, Chris Tomlin and Ed Cash
Arr. James Koerts

With wonder (♩ = 80)

18
22
26
30
34

38
mf
42
46
50
54
f

58
62
66
70
74
ff

(Approx. Performance Time – 2:30)

Indescribable

Words and Music by
Jesse Reeves and Laura Story
Arr. James Koerts

26
31
36
41
mp
47

(Approx. Performance Time – 3:15)

Majestic

Words and Music by Lincoln Brewster
Arr. James Koerts

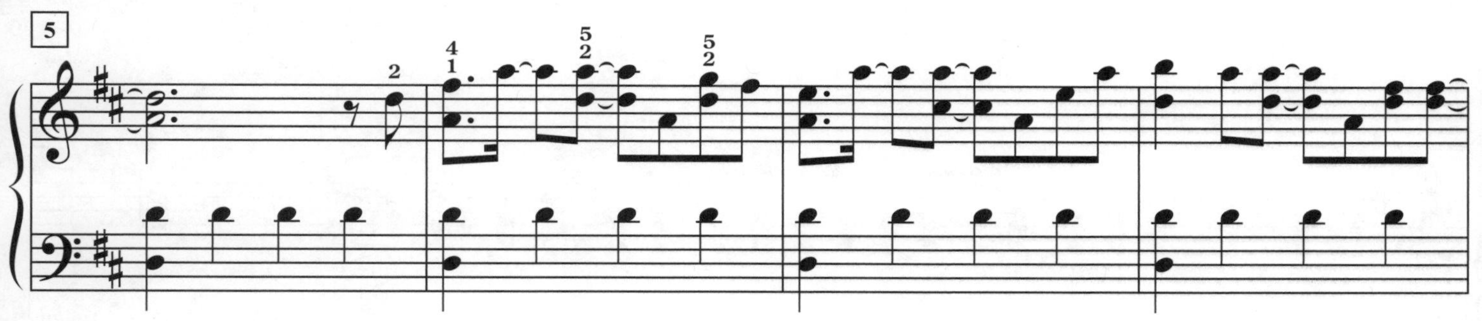

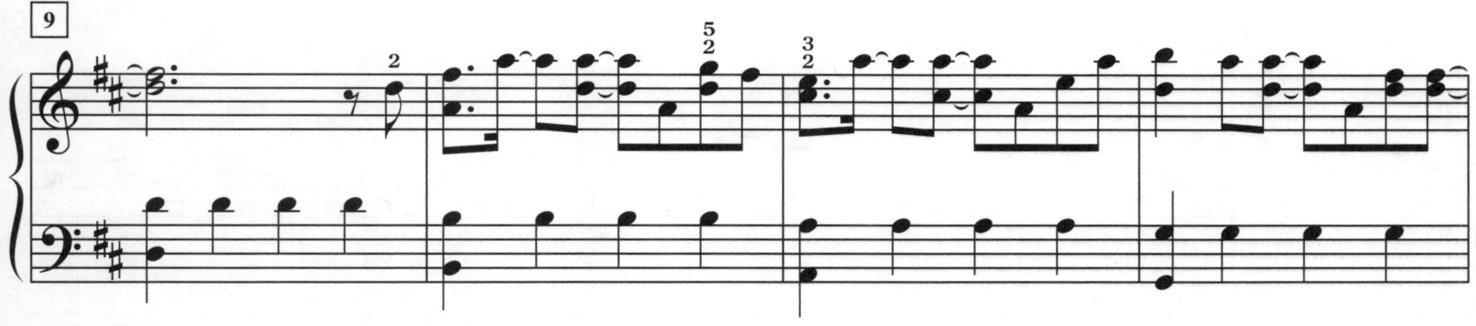

Early 2000s

17
mf
20
23
27
mp
31

34
37
mf
40
43
46

49
5
3
1
mp
5
53
cresc. poco a poco
57
mf
61
cresc. poco a poco
f
65
4
2
1
2
2

69
73
77
81
84
ff

(Approx. Performance Time – 3:15)

Mighty to Save

Words and Music by
Reuben Morgan and Ben Fielding
Arr. James Koerts

13
16
19
22
25

28
31
mf
34
37
f
40

43
cresc. poco a poco
46
ff
49
52
55
mp
8va
rit. e dim.
p

(Approx. Performance Time – 3:15)

Who Am I

Words and Music by Mark Hall
Arr. James Koerts

17

21

p

37
41
45
mp
49
53

57
61
65
mf
69
cresc. poco a poco
73
f

77
81
85
mp
89
93
rit. e dim.
p

(Approx. Performance Time – 4:15)

Worthy Is the Lamb

Words and Music by Darlene Zschech
Arr. James Koerts

Early 2000s

17
21
cresc.
25
mf
29
33

37
41
45
48
52

56
60
cresc.
63
66
69
rit.

a tempo
72
ff
8va
76
mf
f
80
ff
rit.
84
a tempo
mf
88
mp
rit.

(Approx. Performance Time – 3:00)

10,000 Reasons
(Bless the Lord)

Words and Music by
Matt Redman and Jonas Myrin
Arr. James Koerts

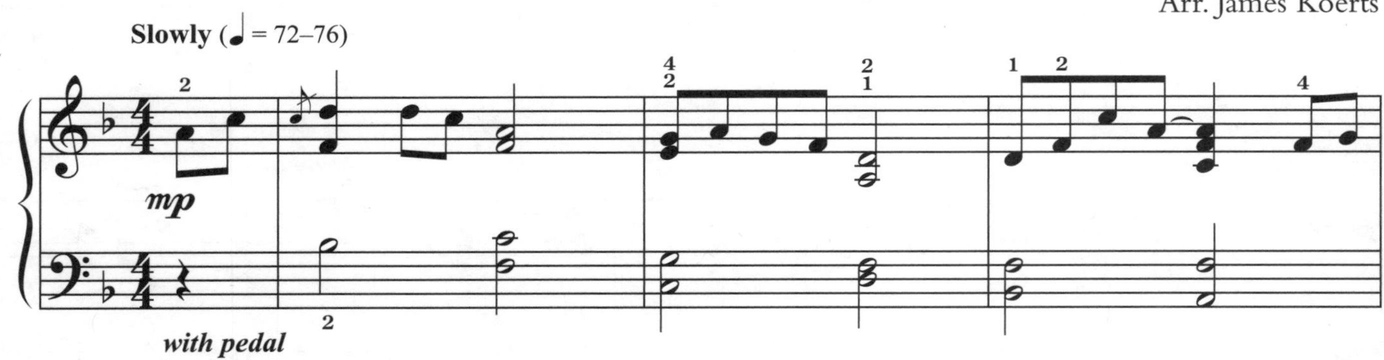

16

19
f
mf

22

26

29
cresc.

32
f

35

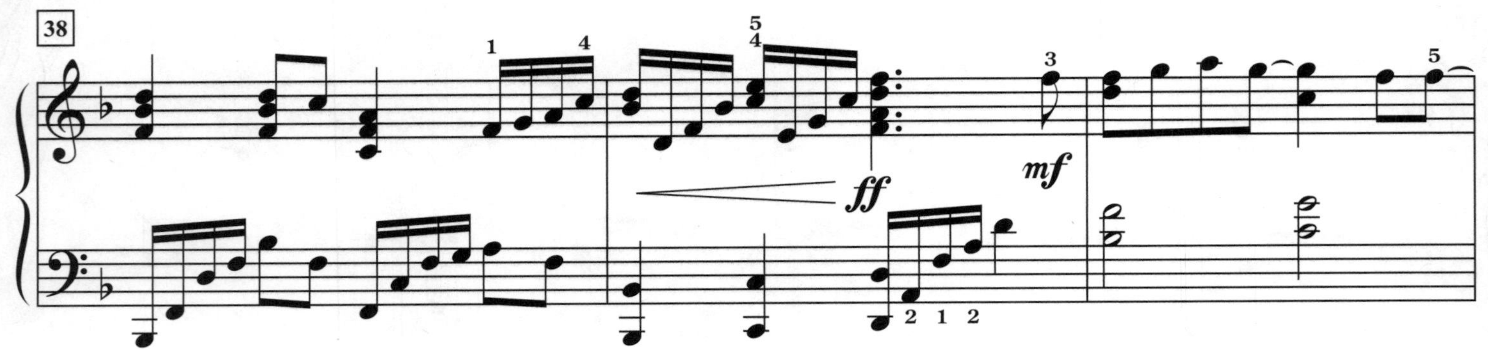
38
ff
mf

41
(5)
1
1 2 4
f
1
5
1

44
1 2

47
1
4
ff
dim. e rit.

50
a tempo
3
1
5
3
5
mf
mp

(Approx. Performance Time – 2:15)

Amazing Grace
(My Chains Are Gone)

Words and Music by
Chris Tomlin and Louie Giglio
Arr. James Koerts

loco
mp
mf
Late 2000s

33
cresc.
f
36
39
42
dim.
p
45
rit.

(Approx. Performance Time – 3:15)

How Can I Keep from Singing

Words and Music by
Chris Tomlin, Ed Cash and Matt Redman
Arr. James Koerts

Late 2000s

13
15
17
19
dim.
21
mp

cresc.
mf

33
35
37
39
41

43
45
mf
mp
48
rit.
50
a tempo
52
rit.

(Approx. Performance Time – 2:45)

I Will Follow

Words and Music by
Chris Tomlin, Jason Ingram, and Reuben Morgan
Arr. James Koerts

13
16
19
22
25

28
31
mf
34
37
40
f

43
46
49
52
sub. p
55
rit.

(Approx. Performance Time – 4:45)

I Will Rise

Words and Music by Chris Tomlin,
Jesse Reeves, Louie Giglio and Matt Maher
Arr. James Koerts

Gently, with expression (♩ = 76)

p

with pedal

17
4
mf
5 2 1 2
20
23
26
mp
3
2 1 2
3 1 2
29
2

33
37
40
43
mf
46

50
4
2
1
54
f
58
repeat optional
5
5
61
64
1.
2.

67
5
2
1
1
3
ff
70
2
2
74
78
81

(Approx. Performance Time – 4:15)

Jesus Messiah

Words and Music by Daniel Carson,
Chris Tomlin, Ed Cash and Jesse Reeves
Arr. James Koerts

Late 2000s

15
19
23
26
29

32
cresc. poco a poco
35
38
mf
41
44

47
51
55
58
61
dim.
mp

64
68
cresc.
f
72
76
80
rit.

(Approx. Performance Time – 3:00)

Our God

Words and Music by Jesse Reeves,
Chris Tomlin, Matt Redman and Jonas Myrin
Arr. James Koerts

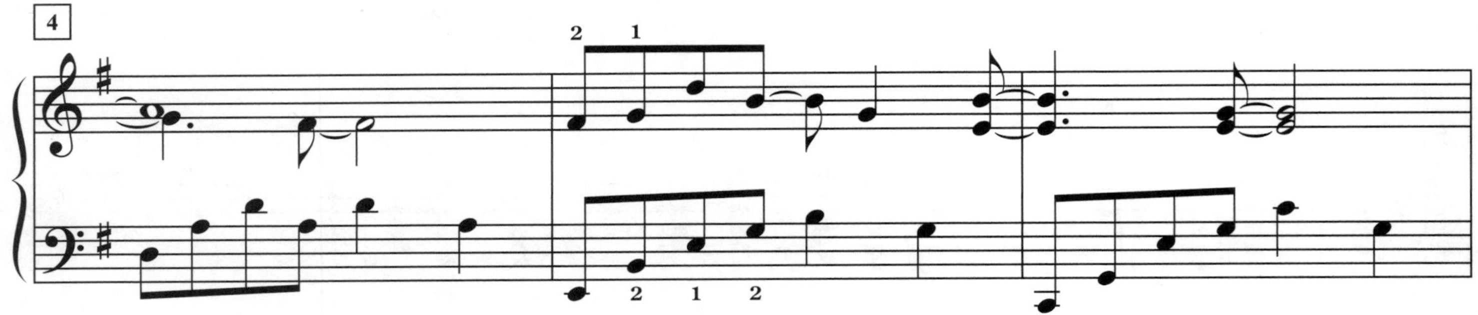

Late 2000s

33
36
40
43
46

49
repeat optional
mf
53
57
mp
60
63
rit.

(Approx. Performance Time – 3:00)

Sing, Sing, Sing

Words and Music by Chris Tomlin, Daniel Carson,
Jesse Reeves, Matt Gilder and Travis Nunn
Arr. James Koerts

21
25
29
33
37

41
45
49
53
57

61
65
4
2
1
5
2
1
f
69
73
77
5
2
1

81
4
2
1
85
89
94
99

(Approx. Performance Time – 2:30)

Your Name

Words and Music by
Glenn Packiam and Paul Baloche
Arr. James Koerts

Late 2000s

15
18
21
24
27
mf

30
33
36
39
42
dim.
p

(Approx. Performance Time – 3:30)

Stronger

Words and Music by
Ben Fielding and Reuben Morgan
Arr. James Koerts

17
cresc.
mf
21
25
29
33

37
41
cresc.
45
f
49
53
mp

57
cresc. poco a poco
61
65
f
69
73
rit.
8va